AR
RL 7.2
Pts. 1.0

understanding mental health

Schizophrenia and Other Psychotic Disorders

CARRIE IORIZZO

Crabtree Publishing Company
www.crabtreebooks.com

understanding mental health

Developed and produced by Plan B Book Packagers
www.planbbookpackagers.com
Author: Carrie Iorizzo
Editorial director: Ellen Rodger
Art director: Rosie Gowsell-Pattison
Project coordinator: Kathy Middleton
Editor: Molly Aloian
Proofreader: Wendy Scavuzzo
Production coordinator and prepress
  technician: Tammy McGarr
Print coordinator: Margaret Amy Salter

Photographs:
Cover, title page: Michael Puche/Shutterstock.com; p. 4:
Nejron Photo/Shutterstock.com; p. 5: Eldad Carin/
Shutterstock.com; p. 6: Jorgen Mcleman/
Shutterstock.com; p. 7: Almagami/Shutterstock.com;
p. 8: Monkey Business Images/Shutterstock.com;
p. 10: Piotr Marcinski/Shutterstock.com; p. 11: Rido/
Shutterstock.com; p. 12: Mopic/Shutterstock.com;
p. 14: IVL /Shutterstock.com; p. 15: Mitar Art
/Shutterstock.com; p. 16: Astudio/Shutterstock.com;
p. 18: Dragon Images/Shutterstock.com; p. 19: Stuart
Jenner/Shutterstock.com; p. 20: Wave Break
Media/ Shutterstock.com; p. 21: Sergey Nivens/
Shutterstock.com; p. 22: Pavel Lysenko/
Shutterstock.com; p. 24: Creatista/Shutterstock.com;
 p. 25: Gladskikh Tatiana/Shutterstock.com;
p. 26: Sint/Shutterstock.com; p. 28: Odua Images/
Shutterstock.com; p. 31: Andrea Danti/
Shutterstock.com; p. 32: Creatista/Shutterstock.com;
p. 33: Prudkov/Shutterstock.com; p.34: Gualtiero
Boffi/Shutterstock.com; p. 36: Monkey Business
Images/Shutterstock.com; p. 38: (left) Alliance/
Shutterstock.com, (right) Dirk Ercken/
Shutterstock.com; p. 41: New Vave/Shutterstock.com;
p. 42: Angela Waye/Shutterstock.com; p. 43: Ollyy/
Shutterstock.com.

Library and Archives Canada Cataloguing in Publication

Iorizzo, Carrie, author
    Schizophrenia and other psychotic disorders / Carrie Iorizzo.

(Understanding mental health)
Includes index.
Issued in print and electronic formats.
ISBN 978-0-7787-0085-2 (bound).--ISBN 978-0-7787-0091-3 (pbk.).--
ISBN 978-1-4271-9398-8 (pdf).--ISBN 978-1-4271-9392-6 (html)

    1. Schizophrenia--Juvenile literature. I. Title.

RC514.I67 2014   j616.89'8   C2013-907642-5
                                           C2013-907643-3

Library of Congress Cataloging-in-Publication Data

Iorizzo, Carrie.
  Schizophrenia and other psychotic disorders / Carrie Iorizzo.
    pages cm. -- (Understanding mental health)
  Audience: Age 10-13.
  Audience: Grade 7 to 8.
  Includes index.
  ISBN 978-0-7787-0085-2 (reinforced library binding) -- ISBN
978-0-7787-0091-3 (pbk.) -- ISBN 978-1-4271-9398-8 (electronic
pdf) -- ISBN 978-1-4271-9392-6 (electronic html)
  1. Psychoses--Juvenile literature. 2. Schizophrenia--Juvenile
literature. I. Title.

RC512.I57 2014
616.89'8--dc23
                                                  2013043866

Crabtree Publishing Company

www.crabtreebooks.com   1-800-387-7650

Printed in Canada/012014/BF20131120

Published in Canada
Crabtree Publishing
616 Welland Ave.
St. Catharines, ON
L2M 5V6

Published in the United States
Crabtree Publishing
PMB 59051
350 Fifth Avenue, 59th Floor
New York, New York 10118

Published in the United Kingdom

Published in Australia
  ...blishing
  ...eet
  ...h

CONTENTS

Schizophrenia and other psychotic disorders are **mental illnesses** that occur in about one percent of the population. Living with a mental illness means living in a society that is not always sympathetic.

The Voices

"I relied on the voices so much, for so long. Without them, I felt a void inside me. Whenever I needed some help, I would start talking to them. And I would get my answers. They gave me whatever I needed to know, be it good or bad. They were there to help me chalk out my plans, to accept survival and how, or whether, to reject it. Without them, without the voices, I couldn't even think about doing anything. I knew I had someone, something, to fall back on...No friends, no contacts..."

— Peter, adult survivor.

Our Perceptions of Mental Illness

Throughout the centuries, people with mental illnesses have been shunned, hidden, forgotten about, and **romanticized**. Peoples' misperception of mental illness was, and still is, associated with severe cases, violence, and bizarre behaviors that are the exception, not the rule. Still, these outdated and misinformed views create great pain for people with a mental illness.

Stigma and Stereotypes

The **stigma** attached to mental illness can keep people from seeking help. Unfounded **stereotypes** can lead to decreased self-esteem and increased symptoms. This can strengthen negative beliefs and cause the person suffering from a mental illness to feel that they cannot control their life. Sometimes the consequences can be deadly. Fortunately, more light is being shed on stigma and, as a result, there is more awareness of the truth about mental illness.

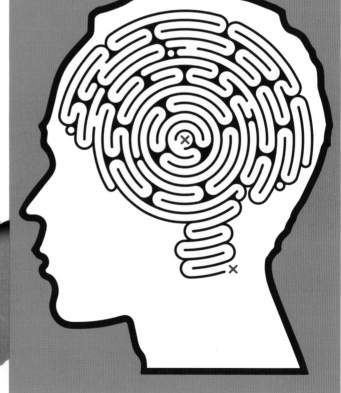

Stigma can make people feel as though they are defined by their disorder and change is impossible.

An Illness of the Brain

Your brain is one of the most complex parts of your body. Scientists are constantly learning new things about how the brain works and how changes in your brain can make you ill. Mental illnesses, or disorders of the brain, can be caused by a change in the physiology, or functioning of the brain, as well as the chemical makeup and structure of the brain. Some mental illnesses are **chronic** and can last a lifetime. Others are episodic, meaning they go away and come back many times over a person's lifetime. Some people have mild to moderate symptoms and others can have symptoms that cause severe disability. The bottom line is mental illnesses can be treated using medication, therapy, or both.

Who Gets Sick?

Mental illness is more common than you think. According to the Substance Abuse and Mental Health Services Administration (SAMHSA), one in five American adults had a mental illness in 2010. One third of these people were between the age of 18 and 25. Unfortunately, only about 40 percent of them, or one in ten, sought help in dealing with their illness. Some estimates say 20 percent of the population will experience a mental health issue sometime during their life. That's about 4.5 million people. Chances are you'll probably know one of them, or maybe you'll experience an illness yourself.

Mental illness is more common than you think.

7

Delusions and hallucinations feel real. You might think you are talking to a person who doesn't actually exist , or believe you are in a relationship with someone, when in fact you aren't.

chapter 1

What Are Psychotic Disorders?

A psychotic disorder is a mental illness in which the major symptoms are delusions and hallucinations. Delusions are beliefs or impressions that a person has that feel real to them, but are not rational and do not in fact exist. Hallucinations are when someone sees or hears something that is not "real" or does not exist. Delusions and hallucinations are also referred to as psychoses. People who are delusional might believe other people are out to hurt them, or believe they are a secret agent or Santa Claus. People who have hallucinations believe they see, feel, hear, or smell things that other people don't.

All in the Family

There are a number of psychotic disorders, including schizophrenia, schizoaffective disorder, schizophreniform disorder, delusional disorder, brief psychotic disorder, and others that occur as a result of a medical condition, substance abuse, or old age. They all involve periods of psychotic or delusional behavior, but differ in their causes, durations, and when they occur. Schizophrenia is the most well-known psychotic disorder and people diagnosed with it usually have delusions and hallucinations that last longer than six months. Brief psychotic disorder usually occurs as a response to a stressful event, such as a death. Substance-induced psychotic disorder occurs in people who use drugs, such as alcohol or crack cocaine, that cause hallucinations.

Schizophrenia

Schizophrenia and schizoaffective disorder are part of the psychotic disorders family. Schizophrenia usually begins in the late teens for boys and the early to mid-twenties for girls. It consists of delusions and hallucinations, and normally follows a traumatic or stressful event in a person's life, such as a death, starting college, or moving out on one's own. A person's speech and/or behavior may be disorganized and their mood or reactions may be flat as though they don't feel anything, or inappropriate as though they feel too much. Although it is rare, young children and youth can develop early onset schizophrenia. It is thought that of all the people who have schizophrenia, only one in 100 developed it before age 18.

"I was both excited and freaked out. My thoughts were huge and nothing else existed. I heard voices through the wall and swooping down on me. They were real to me. I could hear them, even if nobody else could."

— Alia, 14.

Some symptoms of mental illness are noticeable and some aren't. Can you tell whether a person in this picture has schizophrenia just by looking at them? Maybe not.

Signs and Symptoms

Schizophrenia impairs a person's ability to manage their emotions, think straight, and relate to other people. Symptoms vary from person to person, and they can change over time—getting better and getting worse. Symptoms include disorganized thoughts and speech, confusion, strange behavior, mood swings, and loss of interest in hygiene and eating. It takes more than one sign or symptom to diagnose schizophrenia in adults. When diagnosed, the symptoms of schizophrenia are usually broken down into three categories: positive, negative, and cognitive.

Positive Symptoms

Positive symptoms are wild changes in normal behavior. They include delusions and hallucinations, the inability to complete a thought, incomplete sentences when talking, and acting silly at the same time as being distressed.

Negative Symptoms

Diagnosing negative symptoms can be difficult, especially with teens, because some symptoms may be mistaken for normal teenage behavior, such as lack of motivation or being **antisocial**. For a diagnosis to be made, at least two of the following symptoms must be present for at least a month:

- Lack of emotion, facial expression, and eye contact
- Disinterest, inability to speak, and lack of interest in things and people
- Withdrawal from friends and family, being antisocial
- Inability to carry out normal activities such as hygiene, going to school, or making dinner
- Lack of motivation

Cognitive Symptoms

Cognitive symptoms are related to thinking. They can pose the most problems for someone with schizophrenia because they can interfere with daily activities. They include difficulty in remembering and understanding information, and in paying attention or focusing.

What Causes These Disorders?

Scientists don't know exactly what causes schizophrenia and other psychotic disorders. They know that the chemistry and structure of brains of people with these disorders are different. Our understanding of the brain improves every year with new research, but we don't yet know whether schizophrenia is a neurodevelopmental disorder caused by an impairment in the brain's growth, or a neurodegenerative disorder caused by loss of brain function.

Some researchers believe that the cause of schizophrenia has to do with environmental factors that affect your **genes**. The science of epigenetics looks at how the environment makes your genes work, or how it changes or puts stress on how they function. While some people may be at a greater risk than others because of a family history of mental illness, someone else with no family history can still develop schizophrenia or another psychotic disorder.

Stress Factors

When researchers talk about stress factors they mean everything else other than genes, such as the conditions of your birth, exposure to illnesses, nutrition, social life, family environment, drug use, and more. All of these things can cause stress. Scientific studies show that the brains of children and teens are five to ten times more prone to stress than adult brains.

Risky Business

Schizophrenia and psychotic disorders can be devastating diseases that affect your emotions and how you think and express yourself. They can also lead to harmful or risky behaviors.

Smoking is very common with schizophrenia and psychotic disorders, as is substance and alcohol abuse. Schizophrenics are more likely to have severe medical issues such as obesity, high blood sugar, and diabetes because of the types of medications they take. They are more likely to self-medicate, or use drugs, as well. Depression is common as the disease progresses, possibly because of the stigma of schizophrenia and its negative associations.

Stress and stigma can make symptoms worse and sometimes lead people to self-medicate or use alcohol to cope.

Suicide and Psychotic Disorders

Suicide is also a very real risk for someone with schizophrenia and other psychotic disorders, especially after a psychotic episode. Statistics also show suicide ideation, or thoughts of suicide, occurs often within the first five years of the illness or within six months after a hospitalization. Suicide risk is often related to the medications used to control schizophrenic behavior, but substance abuse, depression, and fear of losing mental abilities can also make someone feel like ending it all. About 20 to 50 percent of all people diagnosed attempt suicide at some point in their life. Up to 13 percent succeed.

Our understanding of how the brain functions is constantly being challenged. Brain research helps determine new treatments for mental illness.

Chapter 2

Diagnosis and Treatment

Mental illnesses are physical conditions that don't get better and don't go away without treatment. Although there is no cure for schizophrenia and psychotic disorders, with treatment, you can live a healthy and productive life.

Under Construction

During adolescence, your body approaches a lifetime peak of health, mental ability, and physical strength. Your body, including your brain, is changing. Your emotions are fully functioning, but your ability to keep them in check is not online yet. Your brain is growing and works faster and more efficiently. Yet some of these changes affect the way your body stays healthy. For example, adolescents and teens have a tendency to stay up late, even though getting lots of sleep is necessary for emotional and mental well-being. Many mental illnesses have their beginnings in the growing brain. Understanding how the adolescent brain and body interact, and how the brain grows, can help us understand why brain development can go off track and leave adolescents and teens vulnerable to mental illnesses such as schizophrenia and other psychotic disorders.

What Affects Mental Health?

Good mental health is a balance between all parts of your life: social, physical, financial, spiritual, and mental. As you grow, you learn what is right for you to maintain your unique personal balance. During this growing and learning process, there are many things that can push you off balance and challenge your mental health. Having a mental illness does not make you weird, freaky, or crazy. When your mental health is challenged, it's the same as getting physically ill. Just being an adolescent can throw you off track. This is a time when your body and your way of thinking changes. More responsibility and maturity is expected from you, and this can be confusing and complicated.

"It helps to have an understanding doctor. I have a psychiatrist who I have been seeing for ten years. He understands me and my disorder. Without him and my family, I would literally not be here today. They saved my life."

— Nathan, 27.

Seeing a Doctor

Not everyone notices changes in their thinking or behavior, or may not connect any changes to a possible mental health issue. If you are concerned, you should see a doctor. Most of the time, the first doctor you'll see will be your family physician. To make a diagnosis, he or she will ask you, and probably your parents, questions about your physical and mental symptoms and behaviors, such as if you've been experiencing hallucinations or delusions, or if you've had any recent stressful situations. He or she will also ask you and your parents questions to rule out other types of illnesses and behaviors that can be similar to a psychotic disorder. They will want to know if you have been taking any drugs or drinking alcohol. Alcohol and drug use can affect your mental health. Your doctor should be able to answer your questions about treatment, medications, and their effects.

Take a trusted friend or family member with you to see your doctor. They can help you get the right treatment and support.

Sudden Psychotic Symptoms

Sometimes, if a person has had a sudden psychotic flare-up, they may be taken immediately to the emergency room at a hospital where they will be seen by a doctor or possibly a psychiatrist. A psychiatrist is a medical doctor who specializes in disorders of thinking, feeling, and behavior. The psychiatrist will ask many questions to determine a diagnosis. Schizophrenia can alter brain structure and patterns, so the doctor may order tests such as a magnetic resonance imaging (MRI) or another brain scan. These tests may also rule out sudden brain injuries or tumors as causes of the psychotic flare-up. Child psychiatrists and **psychologists** also treat adolescents and teenagers with psychotic disorders.

It can be frightening to know you have a serious mental illness. Some people find it hard to accept.

Types of Treatments

Your brain is like any other organ in your body—it can get sick just like your kidneys, pancreas, or heart. And just like the rest of your body, your brain can be treated. The main goal of all treatment plans is to lessen your symptoms and even the playing field for you. Some of the more common treatments include drug therapy, counseling, and recreational and social skills training to help get you back into the social circle of friends, family, and school.

Research is showing that some newer types of treatments are also having good results. These include:

- Cognitive Behavioral Therapy—helps to find the things about yourself that bother you. By talking with counselors and setting goals, the way you think and do things can be changed from negative to positive.
- Peer Support Groups—talking and sharing experiences with others in a group helps develop social skills.

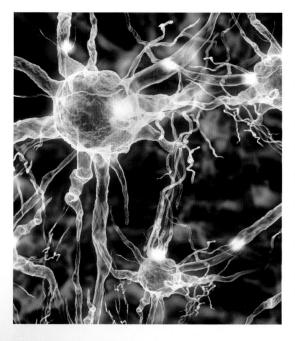

Treatment may be given on an **outpatient** basis. If there is a severe psychotic period, treatment may be given during a hospital stay until you stabilize. Some people stay at in-treatment programs. These group homes or facilities are common for children and youth, especially if the psychosis is serious. When symptoms become less severe, they are treated from home.

Tell It Like It Is

Counseling and therapy are important cornerstones in treating psychotic disorders including schizophrenia. Therapy involves talking to a counselor to identify any negative thoughts and beliefs that make you feel bad about yourself. Once you understand these thoughts, the therapist works with you to change them into positive feelings that increase self-esteem and self-worth. That's why it's important to be honest with your counselor or therapist. Tell it like it is, no matter how crazy it sounds. Your feelings are honest, but the way you act on them may not be appropriate. A therapist can help you recognize the difference. You may also want to mention how your medication is making you feel. Although your therapist can't prescribe medications, he or she can suggest ways to cope or refer you to your psychiatrist for a medication review.

Being honest with your psychiatrist or therapist is important. They are there to help and it is difficult to shock them. There is nothing that they haven't seen or heard before.

Psychotic Disorder Drug Therapy

Psychotic disorders can be successfully treated with medication and counseling. It may take a few weeks for medications to take effect and to notice a change in symptoms. You may also be prescribed different medications, or a combination of drugs, to find out which ones work best. It's also very important to note that once you start taking these medications, you can't just stop. To remain well, these medications must be taken under doctor supervision.

There are two groups of medications that are commonly prescribed for schizophrenia and psychotic disorders. One group has been around since the 1950s and is called typical antipsychotics. They include chlorpromazine (Thorazine), perphenazine (Trilafon), thioridazine (Mellaril), mesoridazine (Serentil), trifluoperazine (Stelazine), fluphenazine (Prolixin), and the most common medication, haloperidol (Haldol). These medications can be taken as a pill or by injection. Some of the side effects are dry mouth, stiffness, sedation, and restless movements.

The second group of medications, called atypical antipsychotics, are more recent and have fewer side effects. They are clozapine (Clozaril), risperidone (Risperdal), olanzapine (Zyprexa), quetiapine (Seroquel), aripiprazole (Abilify), ziprasidone (Geodon), and paliperidone (Invega). Like the first group of antipsychotics, these medications decrease delusions and hallucinations by improving the brain's chemical balance. These chemicals are called **neurotransmitters**. They let brain cells communicate with each other. Drug therapy can also change as symptoms change.

The stigma of a mental health disorder can make the symptoms worse because they put pressure on a person to "act normal" so they won't be ridiculed.

24

Chapter 3

Dealing With Stigma

The dictionary definition of stigma is "disgrace and shame." These are horrible feelings for someone who is already suffering. Stigma is based on misinformation and fear. Mentally ill people, including people who have schizophrenia and other psychotic disorders, have historically been beaten, abused, ignored, stereotyped, and left homeless because of fear and ignorance. Some people believe that having a mental illness is a "lifestyle choice," like choosing to dye your hair blue.

Societal Stigma

Societal stigma is the negative thoughts, beliefs, or reactions that society, or people other than family, have about mental illness. Making negative generalizations and judgments about individuals and groups of people is wrong. Not everyone who has a mental illness is a danger to themselves or other people. Everyone experiences mental illness differently.

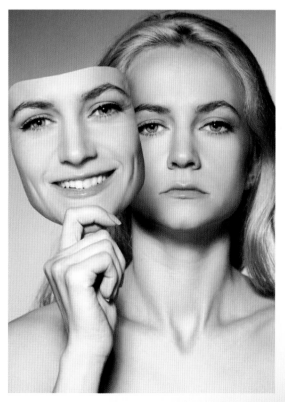

Stigma often forces people to pretend to be someone they aren't so they experience less abuse.

"I have been psychotic, but it doesn't mean I am always psychotic or that I am not worth spending time with because I am 'damaged goods' and can't be trusted. You don't know how hard it is for me to just admit that I have schizophrenia. It's partly because if people know, they just dismiss me as crazy and worthless."

—Dale, 22.

Familial Stigma

Familial stigma is when parents, siblings, or other family members are ashamed or refuse to acknowledge that a family member has a psychotic disorder such as schizophrenia or any other mental illness. It is difficult for children and teens to deal with familial stigma because it makes them feel like they are defective, or at fault for their mental illness. Often, familial stigma can prevent a family member from seeking treatment that can help them get better. It can lead to feelings of self-hate, low self-esteem, and possibly drug abuse, as people attempt to treat their symptoms with drugs and alcohol.

Effects of Stigma

People with mental illnesses can feel like the lowest of the low. They are often treated as though they could "fix" their problems just by thinking positively or being active. Mental illness isn't a fleeting thought. It isn't caused by not thinking happy thoughts. It is a legitimate disease. Even when recognized as a real illness, many people with mental health issues are vulnerable to abuse and to people who would dupe or cheat them. They endure insults and name calling such as "schizo," "psycho," and "incurable." Some lose their families and homes. Other people who are not diagnosed will try to self-medicate with street drugs or alcohol rather than go to a doctor to find out they have a mental illness. Some who have been diagnosed will stop taking their medication and refuse treatment because they want to be accepted by family and friends. Even younger children who have schizophrenia can be **ostracized** because they play or act differently.

Am I Weird?

Mental illnesses can affect anyone. They affect rich and poor, young and old, and people of many different backgrounds and **races**. Psychotic disorders carry with them the added burden of often distinguishable behaviors. When you see someone walking ahead of you, and he or she is talking to themselves and making wild hand gestures, you are likely to think "oh great, just what I need, a crazy person ahead of me." That's an attitude borne out of fear and stigma. Our perceptions of mental illness come from movies, books, and popular culture, where the "crazy person" is also equated with being evil and dangerous. Stigma is also reflected in our stereotypical reactions to the inappropriate behavior of someone who is different. The person who is talking to himself is likely not being treated for his or her illness. Psychotic disorders are very treatable and illness is manageable. Stigma and ignorance are manageable, too.

One way to combat stigma is to stop gossiping and texting about mental illness.

How You Can Stop the Stigma

Stigma goes with lack of knowledge. Take the time to learn about mental illness and don't make judgments on people. Your attitude and actions can make a difference in people's lives and can change the way others view mental illness. Here are a few suggestions:

1. Mental illness isn't a choice. Know that young people, including children, are affected by mental health problems.

2. Mental health disorders often have many causes but the main ones, as with all diseases, are biological and environmental. A person who has a mental health issue is not at fault. Neither they, nor their parents caused the illness.

3. Schizophrenia and psychotic disorders are not a character flaw, or a sign of a weak mind.

4. What you say and how you act are important. Calling people names and spreading misinformed stories about mental illness is wrong.

5. Treat people with a mental health problem the way you would like to be treated. Support your classmates, friends, or family members.

6. Educate yourself and keep a positive attitude. If you find people spreading myths, give them the facts.

7. People who have a psychotic disorder are not necessarily dangers to society. Even if a person's behavior is unusual, they deserve respect. Don't hurl abuse at them.

Acknowledging your disorder and learning to manage your behavior can make you feel better—like you have escaped from a prison in your mind.

Chapter 4

Managing Behavior

Many people with mental illnesses worry about what people might think if they knew. Schizophrenia and psychotic disorders often cause disordered behavior when left untreated, or when treatments are not adjusted to an individual's disorder. Delusions and hallucinations are hard to hide, and psychotic disorders are sometimes thought to be untreatable because of these symptoms. This simply isn't true. But even when these symptoms are controlled, it can be difficult to manage behavior, blend in, and adjust to the norms set by people who do not struggle with mental health. Just as dealing with stigma requires a change in mindset, dealing with and managing behavior and attitudes requires some work, both for the person with the illness and for the people they interact with each day.

In the Know

Stay informed about your illness. That doesn't mean just reading about it, although that's important. It also means knowing how a psychotic disorder affects you personally. Know what triggers a crisis, such as too much stress, being alone too much, heavy workloads at school, or being in a place that is too stimulating or has too many people. Once you are aware of what triggers a psychotic episode, you will be able to manage better and plan for certain events. Having more control makes life much easier.

Support Systems

Having someone you can call when you need to talk can be a great help in keeping your head together. When you start to feel a crisis situation coming on, having a safe **haven** can help you deal with it more effectively. Before you need it, put your support system in place. Tell a teacher, a friend, or someone you trust, what to do in the event of a psychotic episode. Give them your parents' phone numbers, and the name of your family doctor, psychiatrist, and therapist. If there are special things they can do, such as check for medications, take you out of a stressful environment, or remove you to a safe place, this can help you cope with the event.

When you feel as though you are in crisis, turn to your support network for help.

Thought Monitor

Talking it out with your therapist, and using cognitive based therapy skills, can also help you stay on top of thoughts or behaviors that trigger psychotic breaks. Be aware of extreme thoughts, such as "I didn't make the team so I'm a loser." Stay away from negative generalizations, such as "I'll always do bad in chemistry because I didn't get an A on the quiz." Be aware of negative labels that you put on yourself, —"I'm weird." This is you **chastising** yourself or someone else for not living up to expectations.

"For a long time, I felt like my 'mystical visions' were what made me special. My brain has a hard time determining truth, and my visions made me feel fantastic and like I was chosen or anointed. That's hard to give up for the tough reality that most people avoid me and don't think I am special at all."

— Ally, survivor.

Suicide—The Elephant in the Room

Suicide is the leading cause of death among people who suffer from schizophrenia and psychotic disorders. About 40 percent will attempt it once. Males are more likely to attempt suicide than females. People with schizophrenia tend to be more suicidal when they are depressed, when they have a psychotic episode, or when they have been taking their medications for six to nine months. At this time, they are more aware that they have been diagnosed with schizophrenia. If you are having suicidal thoughts:

- Tell someone right away. Your doctor, therapist, friend, parents, or someone else you trust can help you.
- Avoid alcohol and street drugs.
- Remove from your home any objects, such as pills, guns, or a rope that may be used to commit suicide.
- Set realistic goals for yourself and know your limits. Don't set yourself up for failure.
- Avoid negative self-talk. Think positive thoughts. Repeat them several times—hundreds of times if necessary—during the day, every day.
- Keep a schedule and a list of what you need to do each day. This helps keep you organized and your life predictable. Make sure to include things you like to do in your daily To-Do-List.

Tips for Managing Life

- **You are not your illness.** Reject the labels people put on you and define yourself the way you want. You don't have to say "I am a schizophrenic," unless you want to. You don't have to explain yourself at all, if you don't wish to. If you do, you can say "I have schizophrenia," or "I have a psychotic disorder." You can also reclaim words such as "mad" and "mental" and remove their power to shame.

- **Seek treatment.** Medication and treatment can make you feel better. When you feel better, you are in a better frame of mind and physically better able to deal with other people's negativity.

- **Seek support.** Telling a trusted friend, doctor, teacher, or clergy member about your illness can take a big weight off your shoulders. There are people who do understand and care, and who can offer compassion and acceptance.

- **Join a support group.** Having a safe place to go to where there are people who can relate to what you're going through can help prevent loneliness and isolation. Some schools, especially colleges and universities, have Mad Students Societies where students who have experience with mental health issues and care systems can join and support each other. You can even join one if you are not yet college age but are planning to attend college in the future.

- **Start a write-in campaign.** When you see things in the media that put down people with a mental illness or portray them as being different, write in and let them know how you feel.

If you don't have family or friends who can provide support, contact a mental health organization.

Chapter 5

Family and Friends

Having a sibling or parent who has schizophrenia or another psychotic disorder can be difficult, frustrating, and disruptive. Sometimes you may even feel embarrassed and not tell anyone. If your family member is undiagnosed or not taking medication, you may grow up not knowing what to believe, having listened to their delusions and hallucinations.

Parents or Siblings

If you are the one who takes care of your mom, dad, or sibling who has schizophrenia, life can be a difficult balance. You may find it hard to juggle your own duties, school, and friends, and have a social life as well. If your parent is undiagnosed or not on medication, you might have to deal with their delusions, hallucinations, substance abuse, lack of emotions, or seemingly selfish behavior. It may seem like everything revolves around them and their illness, and you are out there on your own.

Feelings of anger, guilt, and pain are normal. You may be embarrassed to bring your friends to the house because you feel they won't understand. As a young caregiver, you need to take time out for yourself to do things that you enjoy. It can help if you have someone—a friend, a trusted relative, teacher, or counselor— to talk to about your feelings. Some mental health organizations have sibling and caregiver groups that meet and offer support and advice to family and friends.

"I love my dad, but I hate what his illness is doing to our family. My mom never has time for me. She's always busy working or trying to manage his life. I know the illness isn't his fault but I sometimes wish he would just be normal or try to act normal. Sometimes I'm so embarrassed, I just can't take it."

—Dawn, 17.

Will I Be Next?

It's understandable that you might be worried that you could develop a psychotic disorder like someone in your family. Statistics say that the risk increases if there is someone in your family who has it. However, it depends on how close the blood relationship is. If your grandparent, aunt, or uncle has a psychotic disorder, there is a three percent chance you will develop it. There is a 10 percent chance of developing psychosis if a parent or sibling has it. If your twin has psychosis, there is a 50 percent chance that you will as well.

STOP

BEING AFRAID

Making and Being a Friend

When you have schizophrenia or a psychotic disorder, making and keeping friends can be challenging. It can also be difficult to be a friend to someone with a psychotic disorder. Many people have a hard time understanding that psychotic disorders are just illnesses. Sometimes there's a lot of stigma to get past before they see the person behind the labels and stereotypes. You might wonder if it's even worth it. But it is. Having a good social network is important to keeping healthy.

To help pave the way for smoother relationships, keep an eye on your moods and behaviors. If you're having a bad day, stay out of the limelight. Avoid situations that might cause a psychotic episode. If you're changing medications or dosages, lay low for a few days until everything levels out. Knowing yourself, and how you react to various situations, can help you build stronger friendships.

A friend is someone who is concerned for you and your welfare. They look out for you and don't use you or abuse you.

Being There for Someone

If you have a friend who has schizophrenia, or another psychotic disorder, you know you can't fix what's wrong. That may be frustrating, but know that just being there and providing support can make a great difference in their lives. You may have been the person he or she turned to for help. People who begin to experience schizophrenia and psychotic disorders are scared of what is happening to them. They may withdraw and isolate themselves without telling you why. It can be very confusing for you that your friend is now acting like someone you don't know. Here are some tips that you can use to become a friend or to make your current friendship stronger.

- *Be reliable.* Let your friend know you're there for him or her no matter what, and that you value his or her friendship.

- *Act calmly.* It's quite possible you may be present during a psychotic episode. Be calm and know in advance what you need to do to get help for your friend.

- *Be sympathetic.* Allow your friend to move at his or her own pace. Appreciate the anger and frustration that he or she must feel.

- *Don't judge.* Your friend has an illness and is working at getting better. Encourage your friend to take his or her medications and follow a treatment plan.

Caregiver Support Checklist

Caregivers, or carers, are usually relatives or friends who provide support to children or adults with a mental illness. Support means many things. It could mean a sibling who looks after a younger or older child. It could mean a youth who cooks, cleans, or ensures an adult takes their meds. The constant demands of caregiving make it a tough job. Caregivers can often feel overwhelmed by many things, including a loved one's diagnosis and the responsibilities they may take on because of it. Children with a parent who has a psychotic disorder may not want to burden their parents by sharing their own fears about the future. Here are some suggestions for understanding your feelings:

1   Know that you cannot always "fix" things or make things better. You are not responsible for the illness.

2   Mental illness isn't a one-way trip. A person can feel better for a while, then feel worse. Not everyone accepts their diagnosis, or wants to make changes to feel better, such as attending doctor appointments or taking meds.

3   Feeling resentful, guilty, frustrated, or angry is normal. So is feeling embarrassed by a parent or sibling's behavior. It is important to talk to someone about your feelings.

4   You may feel fear that you too will develop the disorder. This is normal. Talking to a trusted adult about your concerns can help you feel better.

5   Take up a hobby or sport that is just for you. Exercise helps relieve stress and releases brain chemicals that make you feel better.

Chapter 6

Schizophrenia Toolbox

A schizophrenia toolbox contains a variety of positive plans that can help you handle your more stressful situations. These healthy options will provide you with coping strategies in times of great stress when you are unable to be mindful of your circumstances.

Building Your Toolbox

Your toolbox can be anything from a notepad to an actual box or binder that hold the notes and ideas that you can turn to when negative ideas or situations overwhelm you. Try making a list of at least five positive sayings, ideas, or activities that you can do to make you feel better about yourself. As you progress, keep building your toolbox by adding more and more positive coping skills.

- Call your best friend. BFFs are a great way to boost a negative mood. Talk to him or her and let them know how you're feeling.
- Have a list of positive affirmations or sayings. Something like "I am wonderful!" or "Everyday I am getting better and better." Repeat them, sing them, or whisper them until your mood starts to lift.
- Go for a walk, a run, or bike ride. Exercise can clear your head and create a feeling of balance.

Self-Care 101

When you feel overwhelmed, stressed, or that a psychotic episode is emerging, be gentle with yourself. Think kind and loving thoughts. Don't call yourself names or blame yourself for not being able to control a situation. Remember you are only human and you are learning more and more about yourself every day. Accept that you have this mental illness and remind yourself that it is manageable and treatable. This is a great first step to recovery.

Between episodes, stick to a regular sleep pattern. Research shows that good sleep habits can help reduce psychotic episodes. Eat a balanced diet with lots of fresh fruits and vegetables. Talk to your doctor about taking vitamin supplements. Exercise is a great way to reduce stress and increase self-esteem. Keep good hygiene by showering regularly, having regular dental checkups, and treat yourself to a haircut, pedicure, or manicure, if possible. There's nothing like looking great to feel great.

Raising Your Self-Esteem

Self-esteem plays a huge role in how we feel and treat ourselves. It also affects how we allow others to treat us. Raising your self-esteem can be easier said than done sometimes, but try these ideas:

1   Only hang around people you like and who like you.
2   Avoid people who call you names or make fun of you.
3   Do something you are good at and treat yourself for your successes, no matter how small.
4   Treat people right and with respect, and treat yourself well.

You may also want to set goals for yourself. Start with something small and manageable, like making your bed twice in a row. Reward yourself for your accomplishment. Now set a bigger goal. Keep working your way up the ladder. The sky's the limit.

Being hard on yourself can make your condition worse.

Dealing With Criticism

It's hard to hear people call you names, insult you, and be the brunt of unkind jokes. At times, you may want to be aggressive and start a fight, yell back, or cry. Learn how to express your emotions in a way that keeps you out of trouble and that commands respect. Talk calmly and with authority. Don't yell or name call. Say how you feel honestly and sincerely. Be straightforward. Try to resolve conflict as opposed to escalating it. Be thoughtful and positive, if possible. If you feel you are unable to maintain your composure, walk away—be the bigger person.

Explore Your Creativity

Not everyone is a Picasso, John Lennon, or J.K. Rowling, but that doesn't mean you can't find enjoyment in your creative side. Something as simple as keeping a journal, blogging, or writing poetry can be an outlet for stress. If putting thoughts on paper isn't your thing, try putting them on canvas. Painting can express emotions in color and form in ways you may not be able to say in words. And there's always writing lyrics and singing. Learning to play an instrument or just singing can offer a stress-release mechanism and bring enjoyment and accomplishment to your life. You just might be better than you think.

Activities that do not tax your logical abilities can help you recharge.

Other Resources

It's tough to find good resources on psychotic disorders aimed exactly at the adolescent and teenage group. Most books are written for adults. Check your school or municipal library and, if you can, ask your librarian for help. You can also check the Internet for websites and hotlines. Be careful when searching websites. Not every site gives trustworthy or factual information. Here are some good resources to start with:

Helpful Hotlines

National Alliance on Mental Illness
1-800-950-6264

This is a toll-free (U.S.) 10 a.m. to 6 p.m. (EST) national hotline staffed with trained volunteers who can supply information and support for anyone (adolescents, teens, friends, parents) with questions about mental illness.

National Suicide Hotline
1-800-SUICIDE (784-2433)

This toll-free 24-hour national service connects you to a trained counselor at a nearby suicide crisis center. The service is confidential.

Kids Help Phone
1-800-668-6868

A free, confidential, 24-hour hotline staffed by professional counselors. Supports youths who are in crisis and need help and information on a number of issues. Hotline available in Canada only. Visit their website at www.kidshelpphone.ca

Websites

National Alliance on Mental Illness
www.nami.org

This site provides trusted information on mental illnesses such as schizoaffective disorders, as well as treatment information and where to find support and health. Content is available in English and Spanish.

Mind Your Mind
mindyourmind.ca

An informational teen-oriented mental health site with information on how to get help, as well as personal stories about coping, struggles, and successes, a blog, and interactive tools that can help you identify and cope with your mental health disorder.

Teens Health
kidshealth.org

A safe information source on all aspects of teen health, including mental health. Available in English or Spanish.

Teen Mental Health
teenmentalhealth.org

A useful website on a number of mental health topics for youths, their families, and teachers. The site focuses on evidence-based medicine, with trustworthy research articles.

Glossary

antisocial Not wanting to be social or be around other people

chastising Scolding or reprimanding someone publicly

chronic Something such as an illness that lasts a long time and is difficult to get rid of completely

genes Traits and features inherited from your parents

haven A place of safety such as a refuge or a shelter

mental illnesses Illnesses that cause serious disorder in a person's behavior and thinking

neurotransmitters Chemicals in the brain that transmit nerve signals and messages

ostracized Excluding someone from a group or from society as a whole

outpatient A patient who gets medical treatment without having to stay in a hospital overnight

psychologists Experts in the scientific study of the mind and human behavior; often someone with training in the evaluation and treatment of mental health disorders and illnesses

races Groups of people who share the same ethnic group, culture, history, or language

romanticized Something that is described in an idealized or unrealistic way to make it sound better or more heroic

stereotypes Widely held but unfair or oversimplified beliefs about a type of person or a thing

stigma Shame associated with a particular disorder or behavior

Index